Ask for Wings that Fly

Victoria Ekpo

BookLeaf
Publishing

India | USA | UK

Presentation by *BookLeaf Publishing*

Web: www.bookleafpub.com

E-mail: info@bookleafpub.com

ISBN: 9789357613910

First edition 2023

To my mother, Delia.

ACKNOWLEDGEMENT

All I am, I like to say, I owe to my mother. And it is true. But I do have my whole family to thank for letting me dream and encouraging my writing. I have those who have come to know me well, friends and lovers who gave listening ears and shared interesting stories from their own lives. Thank you to all those writers - stories and poems that have shaped my world, my life and inspired much of my writing.

I am thankful to the universe, for its energy and its enduring presence.

PREFACE

Writing, for me, is a necessity and poetry has saved me many times. Not just the writing but the reading of poetry. In my acknowledgement, I pay homage to all those with the courage to share their work, for in their bravery, many are rescued. Poetry has taught me many things, not least that living is worthwhile and that sharing one's life responds to an invisible law of the universe. The poems in this collection are simple, everyday observations of love, life and friendships. There is nothing personal yet all of it is embodied. You will notice a quiet resistance in some of the poems and a subtle rebelliousness to rhythm, this is on purpose.

I present to you this collection. Read, enjoy and may the poems be whatever you need them to be for you.

A haiku on earth day

Earth, I hope the morning/finds you
glorious again/
faithful bride of God.

A path lined with pine trees

I have been all along

on my way here.

All the lost roads,

the missed signs,

the routes rejected,

others followed

that led down hill,

Up mountains,

dry riverbeds, and

bursting streams.

Lush gardens,

promising forests, dark as the night;

bright skies, full of stars.

A long pathway lined with pine trees,

then you...

The Yes Train (to all the poets at 40+)

We jumped cheerily on and waved the world
away.
To what end, we had no idea and neither did we
care,
Trundling along in delight, shock, awe but
always with glee
We watch the skylines change from blue to any
hue.

The ides of February, then March met the virgins
of the south months,
Not once, not five times but forty, with astute
salutes!
The slender boughs of the Northern plains strain
to kiss
The ample bosoms of their Amazonian sisters,
with success!
Or near enough.

We drift in the fantasies of many sailors,
farmers, makers of things,
And sway to the rhymes of songsters, jesters,
swindlers, players, all!

The stages swing roundabouts as we rush
to laugh,
to cry,
to check our coat pockets and cry foul!

The days merge into yester-nights
And we lose the time to dimes.

Grudges

Today moved ahead
Leaving a debris of memories for you to find.
Will you put them away in the drawer of last
year's discontent?
Or will you file them away with the missing
buttons from last month's disappointment?

I would've loved to pick the lock
On the other day's masquerade
And leave a message where the offending
number was.

Then you'll know I've been
And it'll be another bag of bones
To lug across to the pit you dug for my sins
Two years ago.

Friends

You came at last,
Reluctant like a winter's day
Yet it is spring going to summer
And you drag your feet like it's December.

You need not have made the journey,
You need not have left at all!
You could've remained in your living room
contemplating its high forehead
Or wrapped in your dreams
Negotiating the day with the silence that sits in
your room.

Yet here you are,
Ensconced in my ambivalent company,
pretending to follow my distracted narration of a
wayward day
Keeping you company, going nowhere.

What would you have me do?

Ask how your day was?

I wouldn't want to encourage a response –

A dribble of regret, reticent,

exposing the undersides of your despair.

I know how your day was,

It was here.

Project Design

Build a sign and clarify

What the recipe will verify

For a thing we built up to dismantle

at daybreak in Freemantle.

Don't be tardy, don't be coy

don't be foolhardy or annoy;

Pick the method, decide the rhyme

Say if it will dance or it will mime.

Bring the workers – sayers or nay

Line up the questions, pringles or hay

Draw the diagrams – circles or squares

Make them swirl or instantly pair.

A Gathering

What would you call a gathering of poets?
A band
A babble
A bench
A blush
A bevy
Or a boast?

Some are boys, some are girls,
Some are noisy, some not.
some are judges, barbers, bishops, soldiers,
teachers,
actors, horsemen, lawyers, men?

Maybe they are a syndicate,
A quiz, a shrivel, a slate.
They may rage, but they're not all maidens,
Some are superfluous but not nuns!

If they were all French, we'd call them a peck
Most here are English, maybe a pound?
But the Irish will argue, we are a pint!
And what would we do for the rest of us?

A melody if they all harped,
A poverty if they all piped,
A fagot or roll if they all drummed,
A meter for the percussionists.

We see them in iambs, rhymes, and obscurities,
But I prefer a melody, as in messengers,
Or a worship, as for writers,
A talent, for the gamble they take with their
words,
But most of all, an illusion, for the magic they
bring.

A Birthday

As the heat of the summer
gives way to a golden autumn,
your own years make their orbit
another tally to your great life.

The leaves here, already brown
and while the dew makes steadfast with the
afternoon rain,
the air is expectant with nutmeg and cloves,
Christmas is at the door.
Your new year thrives with the ivy and the holly,
as rich as the elderberry too.

I wish for you now
nothing, less than fullness given,
as full as a harvest in the south,
and peace, as smooth as a clear day in spring.

Taffeta Bride

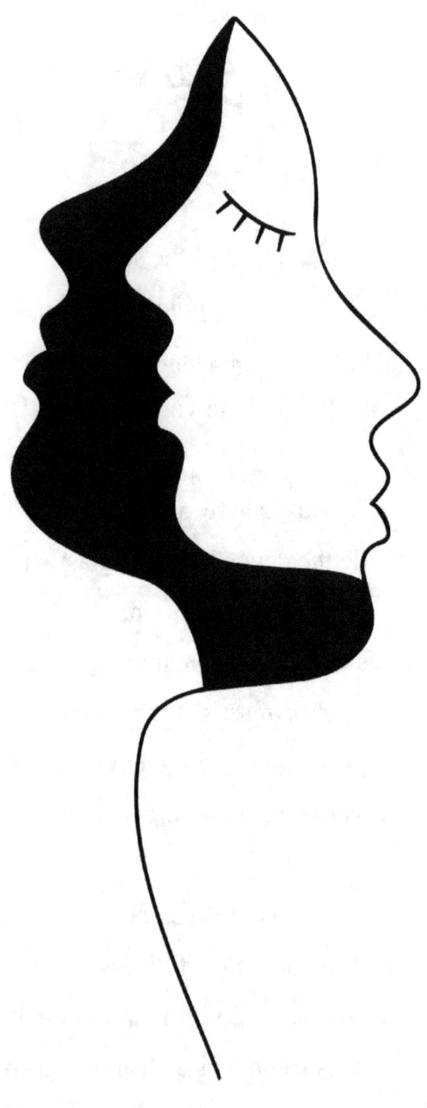

If I love you now,
it is because I've come
to the morning of my senses
and accepted my fate -
which is that I should derail my affectations
and draw the curtains back
from the edge of the wind.

That I should tie
the threads of my imaginations
to the earth beneath your feet,
clipping my inclinations for flight
instead to dream in taffeta,
floating on cotton and silk.

That I should wilt
the expanse of my magnificent wings
and come down to the firmness of your earth
and walk the length of the mile
you've laid in carpets of velvet,
succumbing to the adoration of your fans
assuaged and satiated by wine and meat.

That I should forget
the sensibilities of my ancestors,
and resist the beckoning of my deep blue sea,
the thrusting lust of the forest beyond,
the pressing invitations of the skies above

but lie blindfolded on the shores of your
affection
and wish not for the feel of the wind on my face.

That I should fold myself in,
	Tie myself up,
	Restrain my vision,
	Resist the wind.
	That I should be here and here only,
	That I should die.

But like the brides of your fathers,
you'll see that your suns are tinted
a shade of jade,
and your dreams filled
with the joy of my singing.
If your barns fill up,
it is because I bid it so.
and if you laugh sweet,
I have allowed it.

I will lie in the prison of your arms,
Quietly…,
for otherwise,
you'd die.

The day that came and went

Today didn't hurry,
the cat slept in and
the rain fell slowly, heavily, across the window
panes.
The alarm rang quietly.
The neighbour hadn't yet started his motorcycle
and the wind was low...,
the light, reluctant to come into the room.

I hold you responsible for this faltering,
the ennui that is today.
I hold you guilty for this hesitation,
the foot-dragging afternoon,
the wavering evening...
that did not want to come
yet had to.

Lekeleke

On the great shores of my motherland
a great many birds make homes.
If you ask me to name them all
I'd say, 'let's get a drink'.
For I'll need the night to be long
and a libation to pour
to the spirits of my ancestors.
And when I begin
I'll first count not the largest
but the most steadfast,
and the 'Lekeleke' shall lead the call.

It stands in the tallest of the forest trees,
yet feeds on the backs of the cattle
and escorts the Fulani cattlemen on the long
walk north or south.

It repays the children's call to its magic,
With mystical white dots on their nails
When they sing "Lekeleke give me white
fingers".

Of its coat, there's a flawless white;
Yet it dances not for show
neither does it squawk in pride.

Of its call, a 'Rick-rack'! to soothe the young
And a harsh 'raa'! to the enemy
But altogether quiet the rest,
Solitude at feast and at roost.

Next time you visit my home,
we'll sit in the shade of the almond tree,
sip palm wine tapped from my neighbour's tree
and watch the skies.
When the egret swoops across the way
we will bear witness and sing:
"Lekeleke give me white fingers";
Children again.

Carrot Soup

An orange footpath

wound around the base

of the sky,

muddy,

a patch of ice here and there.

Were you a meal laid

for a maiden in the South,

you'd be carrot soup;-

creamy yet knobbly,

a hint of chilli pepper,

crowned with an island of bacon.

Delusions in Turquoise

Write to me
Of sunsets and blue seas.
Write to me,
Of lost loves and Boleyn teas.
Write to me,
Of encounters in strange streets
And I'll give to you
A handful of tricks and treats.

Set for me,
A picnic of wine and berries.
Set for me,
A bed made with silk ties,
Set for me,
A train of sunken grass in grace,
And I'll give to you
My body, wrapped in myrrh and lace.

Lie to me,
Of days spent in dreams and dew,
Lie to me,
Of evenings filled with passion and clue,
Lie to me,
That you'll love me till the end of time,
And I'll give to you,
My heart sold in gold and thyme.

A summer prematurely here

The storm blew the skies wide open
And the sun spilled for days on end
Disturbing the equilibrium of the winter
morning
Making us dream of summer heat
urging our desires prematurely ripe.

On the train North,
the open fields promise of dryness
the fecklessness of an English drought,
While the distant towns belie
The frantic rant of a winter day,
Suddenly turned warm and bright.

But I know very well that

As soon as we round the bend

That brings us firmly north,

The winds will smack us right in the face

And spit all that rain back

Over our deluded heads.

An ode to the signer

Hands,...

all heart and soul and mind and goal

speaks of wonders young and old

a world quiet as a summer foal

magical even as an evening unfolds.

Face,...

a message along the lines

on the lips speak along

a silent refrain of poetry and song

a miracle in the dance of her eyes and mouth.

A Promise

Like winter trees I await, patiently
your springtime
embrace.
A breath held
a hand suspended
that space between autumn and spring
where everything happens, yet we wait.

                        I wish the

moment when your love

                        meets mine
                        to fly like birds,

in the direction of our journey;

looking up, not looking back…
I'll hold your hand
Steadfast*
So that if the bottom falls
out of your heart,
you'll not be alone.
And all can be said in the vacuum where we
waited all those years,

                        not holding

hands.

Love, be not lost

Love be not cold or hot or lukewarm,
be not a cloudy moonlit night on a summer's day
parading with hope not yet fully formed
or a shallow stream iced over in winter's breath.

Be not distant, claustrophobic, degraded,
disgruntled or old
or erratic in youth's great angst and irritation.
Be not distracted, listless, forlorn
intense, clutching, fretful, keen.

Be not a thousand air miles on a rickety flight
or a bereft, shingly beach at the end of a storm,
lacking expectations, surrounded by palms
lapping brown water, frothy with shame.

Be not forgetful – a neglected pot of tea on a
cold day
Cooling milk, encrusted with cinnamon
Abandoned at a table intended for company.

Be not here, yet elsewhere
insecure in the talent of the day's encounter.
Wistful, itinerant, nomadic, tormented,
Seeking a sorrow left on a footpath, a long way
back.

Be not these,
or like those pallets stacked in the alleyway –
free of their burdens
Empty of purpose, fearful of time.

If you could and would
Come like two dozen shooting stars
Lost sometime in the din of things
But now found on a quiet spring hill,
Readily here.

Gathered Up

Of all the things gathered up,

You came down to me.

Push and pull through the storms you did,

To get through to the other side of the drought.

Of all the things gathered in,

You lost your way with me,

Backwards and forwards down the street,

You went,

To get to the point where we held hands and ran.

Of all the things gathered high,

Smooth and tough and warm and short,

You came and went without a clue,

Into the sunset and the blue.

We are the countryside

We are this earth,
All fields and moors, mounds, hills, mountains
All rocks and crags, jagged cliffs – sand and grit.

The sky and space
Waters – big and small
Trickles to waterfalls
Babbling brooks, gurgling streams, angry rivers,
and endless seas.

We are caretakers,
Custodians of paths laid by history,
Kept in protest and work,
Farmers, walkers, folds …
A toll-free access for all and all.

We are witnesses,
Of the daily dance of the English climate
Daffodils early and late, bluebells that dazzle the
sight.
Trees in slow-motion – dressing, undressing,

A landscape quickly changed, in snow, storm,
sun or inevitable rain.

     We are meeters and greeters,
That first brush with the open air,
A nod, a smile, a welcome wave
The understanding of togetherness in this.

     We are the countryside.
You, me, and that fellow that scoffs at the rain.
For what is a meal if not the child of the soil?
What is your soul if not a star in the sky?

     We are the land,
Wrapped in the promise of its care.
Freed by its generosity
Given control in trust,
To roam, to tend, to be.

We are the countryside.
You, me and every fellow here.

Mercy, Mercy

When the brook is dry and the mountain high
And all our fears together lie;
Then will mercy form us,
Then will mercy fill us,
Then will mercy come.

When the beatings of wings, the thrashings of
legs,
The gnashing of teeth grinds our bones to dust;
Then will mercy hold us,
Then will mercy enfold us,
Then will mercy come.

When all our tears together form a flood
And the paths we knew lead nowhere clear in
sight,
Then will mercy hear us,
Then will mercy bear us,
Then will mercy come.

If time a trick plays to confuse our hearts and
drag our hopes astray,
If sorrows beset our souls and darkness endures
unkindly long,
If grace is late, our strength wane,
Then may mercy attend us,
Then may mercy keep us,
May mercy come.

Ask for Wings that Fly

On a winter's walk,
Green muddy fields that yield next year's fruit,
A heavy sky without relief-
Seagulls but no fish.
Count not the despair of each step
Nor invite the growing depression of the tide,
Press on to the higher ground
And ask for wings that fly.

If adversity refuses the chiding of our
enthusiastic hearts-
We must our faiths rewind, dancing furiously in
the wind; -
Arms raised, face to the sky
A force to behold in word and deed.
We will take a breath and slow the fear
And ask for wings that fly.

As for the profiling doubts
Marshall them to the goal
Deliberate, simple acts
Of mindfulness, all of the time.

Love, be loved,
No expectations of the gain.
Kindness, here, reticent, and true
And ask for wings that fly.

Ask for a kind sun and for a storm that embraces
you like a child,
Ask for the ascent to be kind to your knees and
for woods that smell of rain;
Ask for renewing clouds and uninterrupted
views,
For solitude and birdsong that murmur in the
stream;
Ask for peace with no disruption to the flow,
Ask for wings that fly.

www.ingramcontent.com/pod-product-compliance
Lightning Source LLC
LaVergne TN
LVHW010913200726
843509LV00013B/1925